Queen Breeding for Amateurs

Queen Breeding for Amateurs

© C. P. Abbott

ISBN 978-1-904846-50-5

Cover picture: Courtesy of John Phipps

This volume was first published by Bee Craft Ltd. in 1947. Beekeeping at that time had benefitted from the war time arrangements for the supply of sugar and the book filled a popular need, for the many new beekeepers which resulted in a reprint of the revised 1951 edition in 2010.
With the present interest in beekeeping and the need once more to breed more queens, this reprint of Abbott's second edition has been reproduced, with the support of his family.
It should provide a valuable addition to the literature.

Northern Bee Books
January 2010

Published by Northern Bee Books
Scout Bottom Farm
Mytholmroyd
Hebden Bridge HX7 5JS (UK)

QUEEN BREEDING
FOR AMATEURS

By

C. P. ABBOTT

B.B.K.A. Expert and Examiner,
Chairman, Ealing and District Bee-keepers' Association.

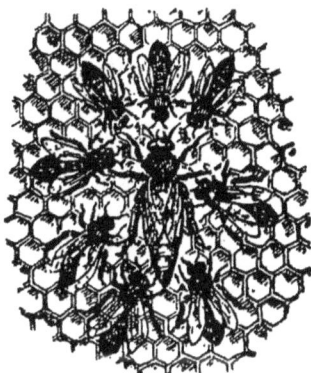

ILLUSTRATED WITH PHOTOGRAPHS
BY THE AUTHOR

First published 1947

New and revised Edition
1951

Northern Bee Books

FOREWORD

Three-quarters of a century ago Charles Nash Abbott founded the first British bee periodical. His grandson carries on the family tradition in giving the craft this short treatise.

Commercial producers of queens have been fairly adequately provided for by writers on both sides of the Atlantic. Mr. Abbott is obviously acquainted with their technique, but realises that the smaller honey producer needs methods suited to his skill and circumstances. He accordingly gives plain advice and simple instructions which the amateur will not find beyond his grasp. The author's illustrations are admirable in making clear the text.

H. J. WADEY.

CROWBOROUGH,
   SUSSEX,
      March, 1947.

ACKNOWLEDGMENT

Firstly let me acknowledge my indebtedness to the many writers on Queen Breeding from whose works I have learned so much, and then thank those who have kindly read my manuscript and helped me to revise it, especially Messrs. Manley, Wedmore, Dingle and Wadey. Let me also remember my grandfather, C. N. Abbott, who was a pioneer in bee literature for the small bee-keeper; to him I feel I owe the inspiration to try to help others in the craft.

C. P. ABBOTT.

SOUTHALL,

   March, 1947.

SECOND EDITION

I must thank all those who have expressed their appreciation of my first edition, for it is their kind recommendation that has created the need for a second one. I must also thank those who have written to me offering suggestions for improving the book.

I can only hope that this new edition with the revisions and additions I have made will further encourage the work of my fellow amateurs.

C. P. ABBOTT.

SOUTHALL,

   January, 1951.

CONTENTS

Chapter I

THE VALUE OF SELECTIVE BREEDING

MAN has domesticated all kinds of livestock, and so has produced strains which are entirely dependent upon him for their survival; hence it has become necessary for him to breed animals especially suited to the purpose for which they are to be used, and at the same time suitable for the environment in which they have to live. We should not assume that stock is only bred for its high productivity, for in many cases it is environment which is the deciding factor.

Whilst the greater part of this selective breeding has been done by professionals, amateurs or back-yarders have done a great deal to improve the quality of the stock they keep. Yet the amateur who keeps a few hens or some other kind of livestock is not of necessity a breeder too, for he can easily replace his stock by the purchase of pedigree birds or animals from the expert breeder.

Most of our amateur bee-keepers are, however, both bee-keepers and bee-breeders; but unfortunately too few of them give any thought to the improvement of the stock they keep. On the other hand, the commercial man whose livelihood depends upon his bees gives a great deal of thought to the breeding of better stock, and many of them buy large numbers of queens from professional breeders if they are unable to produce enough of their own.

Good queens can be bred by any bee-keeper who has passed the beginner stage, and who has learned something about the ways of our bees from the simpler text books and from association with his fellow bee-keepers.

Most of our books on bee-keeping only devote one chapter to queen breeding, and too often that chapter deals with the grafting of larvæ in artificial cell cups, a method which is neither necessary nor advisable for the small breeder; hence not enough attention is given to the more important points which are essential in the breeding of good queens.

When I first became interested in queen breeding, I found it was necessary to read a great many of the excellent books written by experienced breeders, before I could feel that I had a grasp on the subject. Some of these books are no longer easily obtainable, and even if they were, I doubt whether the average bee-keeper would wish to sift all the knowledge contained in them; much of it is not of great interest to the amateur.

By trying to breed better bees we can make a real contribution to the work of those who are trying to improve our strains, and so for the help and encouragement of my fellow amateurs I have written this little book containing, as far as I know, nothing that is new, but merely summarising those principles which are generally accepted as desirable in the production of good queens. I write as a humble student, rather than as an expert, for the longer I live with my bees, the more I realise how limited is our knowledge of them and their ways.

Before we discuss how to produce a good queen, we must consider the selection of the strain from which we intend to breed; this may well be the most difficult aspect of the subject, yet it is surely the most important one, and the one in which we must forever try to gain experience.

Although there are many good books which deal with genetics, or the laws of heredity in animal breeding, far too little is known about this important subject. There are still wide differences of opinion amongst those who make a study of it. The amateur breeder should find it interesting to read something about this subject, but he will find it quite satisfactory to carry on with the knowledge that in all stock breeding the characteristics of the parents are, to some extent, handed down to the offspring, so that the child does, in fact, take after its father, its mother, or both.

This means that we can " breed in " any particular quality,

good or bad, by constantly breeding from those parents *which have the ability* to pass on those qualities to a marked degree. But it is equally important to remember that we can " breed out " the qualities we do not desire by refraining from breeding from those animals which are found to pass on such undesirable qualities.

Inheritance takes place through hypothetical units called genes, and it is known that there is some linkage between certain of them ; if this is so, we would expect to find that if a child has inherited one particular quality from its parents, it would automatically inherit certain other qualities which are " linked " with it. So far as I know, no such linkage has been found in bee-breeding, but it is worth while to be on the look out for some evidence of it in our queen breeding operations.

A queen is not necessarily a good queen just because she is a pure Italian, or because someone has given her a fancy name. Some countries enjoy a climate which is very suitable for queen rearing, and no doubt the best breeders in those countries do, by careful selection, produce large numbers of excellent queens. It does not follow that these queens are bred for their suitability to our environment.

The mongrel bees we normally keep are the descendants of many strains and races of imported bees, but they have to some extent become acclimatised, or naturalised.

We may like to think of them as " hybrids " but we should understand that a hybrid is really a first cross between two pure races. If we breed from hybrids the progeny will inherit the qualities of either or both parents but the mongrel with its mixed ancestry may give a greater variety in its offspring.

Before we decide to experiment with bees imported from other places, let us see what we can do to improve the native bee that we keep in our own back garden, or should I say apiary ? We must realise that because of their ancestry numbers of their progeny will not be true to strain but we know that by constantly selecting the good and rejecting the bad we begin to fix the qualities we wish to keep. Even pure bred strains will not remain pure unless they are constantly bred by selection and after all, these mongrels of ours, have many of the good qualities we need and some of these qualities may well have become " fixed " to a certain degree in the process of becoming acclimatised.

Chapter II

WHAT TO SELECT

THERE are many qualities we may wish to " breed in " or to " breed out " of our bees, but we should give some little thought to our needs so as to be sure that we are working for those that are the most desirable.

Docility. I put this quality first because I think it is a most important one. There are many good reasons, firstly because I don't like stings myself, secondly because we live in a rather crowded island and should give some thought to our neighbours, to whom vicious bees can be such a nuisance. My third reason is because of our beginners ; we were all beginners once, and can make life much easier for those who follow us if we see that they can make a start with bees that are easy to handle.

Are vicious bees better honey getters than docile ones ? Many people will say yes. Most of the books say that it need not be so. I may say that the best honey crop I ever had came from the most docile colony in the apiary. Most of the experts I have met seem to think that bees can be too docile, and that extremely docile bees are not good enough honey getters, but I have yet to convince myself that this fault was due to their docility. There can be no doubt that it is possible to breed bees which are good workers, and yet are not unduly vicious.

In my experience, vicious bees never improve, their nasty ways spread to other colonies ; so if you are one of the tougher sort who likes a bit of temper in his bees, be a good neighbour, and don't let it go too far.

Prolificacy. Do we want prolific bees ? Most of us admire the queen that produces those fine large slabs of brood, and, too easily jump to the conclusion that those are the queens from which to breed. It is true that we want plenty of bees if we are to get honey, but we only want them at the time when the nectar is available in our particular district. There are many places where a prolific strain of bee can never get enough nectar to keep itself and yield a surplus.

Every single bee that is bred has its cost—it costs our bees both honey and bee labour to breed it; it consumes honey for its own maintenance; it is no uncommon experience for a colony to die out in June from starvation, unable to find enough food to keep itself alive. I think we should aim to breed longer living bees, for then we could have our stronger colonies of foraging bees with a lower cost in terms of food consumed in breeding them.

Colour. Colour in itself can have but little value, yet I suppose more queens have been selected for colour than for any other single quality. Bee-keepers have tended to ask for golden or yellow queens, and breeders have bred to meet that demand, but is colour in itself a virtue? It is an easy quality to select for. It may be evidence that a queen is pure mated and has mated to one of the selected drones, but it is not evidence that the progeny will have inherited those other qualities for which we are breeding.

We may yet find some indications that other qualities are genetically linked with colour; that is to say that if a bee has inherited the colour, it will also have inherited some other qualities with it, but so far there is no evidence that this is so.

Colour is affected by environment, for it seems that in this country yellow bees tend to get darker than they would if bred in warm climates. This does not mean that there is any genetic change in them.

Swarming. Most of us would wish to breed out any excessive tendency to swarm, but no doubt the extent to which we do this will depend upon the particular breeder's methods of management.

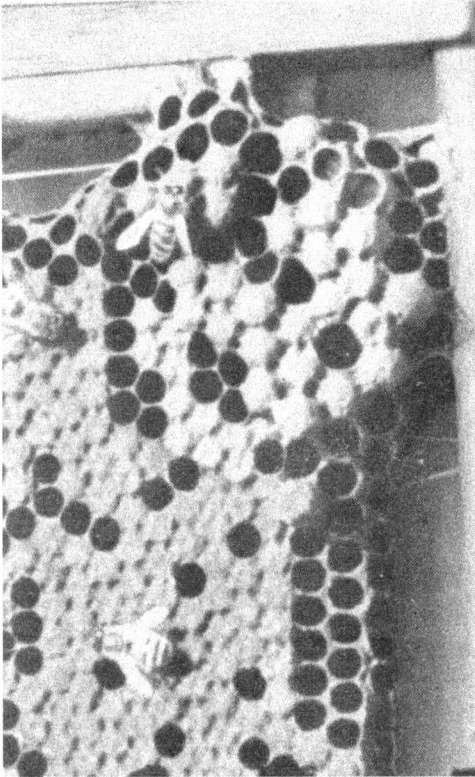

A PATCH OF DRONE BROOD. Such patches should be destroyed unless they are drones of selected strain.

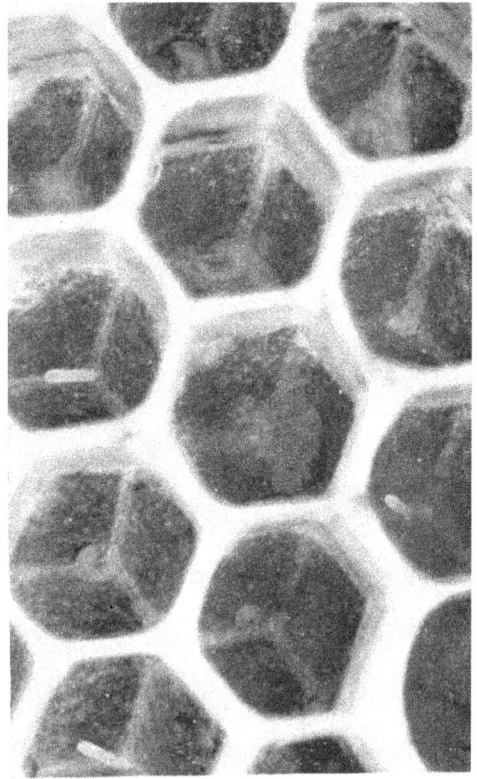

EGGS AND NEWLY-HATCHED LARVAE. The photo does not show much larval food. The comb has been away from the hive for some considerable time.

AN EMERGENCY CELL built on the midrib where the worker egg was laid.

SWARM BOX with the wire gauge bottom. The slot in the lid enables the selected comb of larvae to be inserted; the slot is then closed with the wooden strip.

A SCREEN BOARD. Useful in queen – rearing for confining bees for cell – starting; also useful to provide adequate ventilation when moving bees.

Those who try to keep bees in an ordinary single brood chamber will no doubt breed to keep the swarming fever as low as possible, whilst those who practise some of the swarm control methods, may not notice any tendency to swarm. I have played about with most of the fancy ideas in my time, but have now settled down to the simple life. I keep my bees either on a brood chamber and a shallow, or on the old 14 in. by 12 in. deep frame.

After that I rely on mother wit to smell out the odd hive that is going to swarm, but must admit she doesn't always work, so I get a few swarms. I am doubtful if swarming could, or should be bred out entirely, but I don't breed from queens that have swarmed.

Disease Resistance. Bees have been bred for their resistance to foul brood, and there is no doubt that some bees resist disease better than others. I am told that American queens show very little resistance to acarine, as that disease is unknown in the U.S.A. It would seem, therefore, that those who have the misfortune to have disease in their apiaries might do well to breed from those bees which showed resistance to the disease, and who knows, but that one day we may find this a better way of combating disease than those methods we employ at present.

Some Other Thoughts. We can breed bees which are good cappers if we are working for sections; we can also find those with longer tongues who can reach nectar which is inaccessible to their shorter tongued sisters. Some strains seem to work longer hours than others; bees have been selectively bred to use no propolis; and again, there are those which remain quiet on the combs when we are handling them. I have heard the old black bee credited with being economical in winter stores, but I doubt if we can really expect to find a strain which has this quality, for it may have been due to the fact that being less prolific, there were fewer of them.

I think most bees will winter well provided that they are young bees with adequate stores, and if there are not enough young bees to winter, it is more likely to be the fault of the bee-keeper than any fault of the queen. I believe that most queens will lay all the eggs you want provided they are allowed to keep the food they need, and have enough nurse bees to tend the brood which they can produce.

Chapter III

HOW TO SELECT

The Breeder Queen.

IN the amateur's apiary there may not be many queens from which to select our breeder. We will naturally select one whose progeny has the qualities we most desire and one which lacks the vices we might wish to eliminate, but that is not quite enough, so this point must be especially noted :

We also need a breeder who is capable of reproducing herself. Her daughter queens must be as good as their mother.

A queen carries in her the genes of both her mother and the drone that mated with her mother. She produces queens that contain not only her own genes, but also those of the drone or drones that mated with her. It is now generally accepted that during her mating time a queen may mate with more than one drone ; it may be that only one of these matings is effective, but opinions differ on this point. Until it is proved to the contrary, therefore, we may assume that if a queen has mated with two drones she will lay eggs with the genes of either of her mates. Presumably our ideal breeder will be a queen who has only mated with one drone, or if it has indulged in dual mating, then it is to be hoped that both of the drones are of the same strain. The age of the breeder is not so important, for it seems clear that mere age does not affect a queen's ability to pass on her hereditary qualities ; if, however, she is really worn out, the stamina of her progeny might be affected.

How can we amateurs in our back-yard apiaries hope to find these breeder queens who have mated to the proper drones ? Let us look for a colony headed by a proven queen, and where there has been one or more natural supersedures, and where, in spite of the fact that the original queen has been superseded, the daughter appears to have the good qualities of her mother. This would tend to show that the original queen was satisfactorily mated, and would encourage us to hope that the daughter too had mated with the right drone.

At least one eminent expert says that queens generally mate with drones from the colony or nucleus from which they take their mating flight. This seems to be quite logical.

If this is so, then in a hive where there has been a natural supersedure, there is an odds-on chance that the virgin will have mated with a drone or drones from the same hive, which should give us a start in fixing the strain that we wish to breed.

It may be thought that this is close inbreeding, but this is not so, for the drone and the queen, although born of the same mother are not in their genetic make-up, brother and sister; there is, as it were, a generation between them due to parthenogenesis. Inbreeding is regularly practised in order to fix desirable qualities, and animals are often mated which are much more closely related than the queen and the drone, and tremendous improvements have been made in stock bred from these related parents by constant selection of the subsequent breeding pairs.

I do not advise the amateur to start by purchasing some fancy breeder queen from an outside source, for he should first try to improve his own strain by careful selection from his own apiary. When he has gained some experience he may find it possible to improve by the importation of new blood of known suitability, but do not assume that a bee that does well in some other district is going to be a better bee for your purposes.

Selecting the Drone.

All breeders agree that the selection of the drone is just as important as the selection of the queen, in fact, some suggest that it is even more important. Drones fly for great distances, so it is difficult to ensure that only the selected ones will be flying in the amateur's apiary.

We read of isolated mating apiaries where none but the selected drones are flown, which sounds all right in theory, if such isolated places can be found. I wonder if there is anything so perfect in this imperfect world?

Whilst we amateurs may sometimes find an isolated spot where we can mate queens without too much intrusion from strange drones, let us not despair if we have to take things as we find them, and put up with the neighbouring bees.

We can pin our faith on those writers who say that the majority of matings take place with drones from the same hive or nucleus from which the virgin is mated. I know that this is disputed, and can only say that I have found that in an ordinary supersedure, or when queens are mated from the parent colony the bees in subsequent seasons generally seem to show the same qualities, good or bad, as the parent stock.

In my view, therefore, the best thing to do is to try and use the drones in the colony of the breeder queen in the first year, and with the queens so bred re-queen all the colonies in the apiary. Some of these first year queens will not have mated to our selected drones, and so will be cross-mated; it is said—it may be a biological fact—that cross-mated queens will still produce pure drones as the drone is born of an unfertilised egg and carries none of the qualities of the drone that mated with his mother, but only those of his grandfather. This might lead us to assume that having re-queened our colonies in the first year with queens bred from our breeder, all the drones in our apiary would be of the breeder strain. Do not rely on any such assumption; there is far too much uncertainty. There must always be a great deal of uncertainty as to the purity of any drone, and there is always that possibility of dual mating which would mean that the queen was producing two or more strains of drone. We must keep on selecting the drones as well as the queens, by studying the characteristics of each generation.

We can, if we wish, increase the number of selected drones in our apiary by encouraging suitable colonies to breed drones, either by giving them a frame with drone base foundation, or by allowing them to have a few combs with large patches of drone cells ; combs which we would ordinarily get rid of in working colonies.

We must also suppress the production of undesirable drones by limiting the amount of drone brood in the hives that produce them, and if need be by trapping and destroying such drones during the mating period. We should also avoid bringing home odd lots of bees—swarms and such things—even though it is tempting at times to use them to make nuclei. I am sure I once imported vice into my apiary in this way, and subsequently had quite a job to eliminate it.

We can help ourselves, too, by helping our neighbour, and letting him have some of our selected queens, for the more we spread these queens in our own neighbourhood the less likely are we to be troubled with undesirable drones.

So it will be seen that I am advocating that we should start breeding as far as possible from the queen and the drone in the same parent colony.

It must be remembered that the drone is not potent until thirty-seven days after the egg is laid, but queens may be ready to mate eighteen days after a cell is started. From this it follows that the eggs which are going to produce our selected drones must be laid nearly three weeks before we start our queen breeding operations.

Chapter IV

FOUR STAGES IN QUEEN BREEDING

AS the egg is transformed into a virgin queen, it passes through many phases, but for our purposes we can think of them under three periods of time :—

Incubation of the egg ... ... approx. 3 days
Feeding the larva ... ... approx. 5 days
Spinning, resting, and transformation approx. 7 days

the queen emerging on or about the 16th day.

These times are only approximate ; they vary considerably according to temperature, the food available, and no doubt for other reasons.

During its incubation period, it would seem that the egg receives no attention from the bees, but immediately before it hatches some larval food is placed around it ; in fact, there is some doubt as to whether the egg will hatch at all if this food is not present. This treatment of the egg is not under our control, so we may say that queen breeding only starts when the egg hatches.

But from the moment that the egg does hatch, the queen breeder is concerned, not only for the thirteen days to the emergence of the virgin, but beyond that to the final mating.

Although we divide our queen breeding operations into four distinct stages, most amateurs will do the job in two or three ; nevertheless we must understand that those four stages are :—

STAGE 1 : ACCEPTANCE OR STARTING

Acceptance is the term generally used when the bees have accepted a grafted larva as a potential queen. When a larva of suitable age is given to bees in the right condition, and, if it is accepted, a cell will be started in twelve to eighteen hours.

The evidence of acceptance is clearly visible, for the bees will have started work on the cell cup in which the larva was grafted and the larva will be seen to be " floating " in a bed of larval food.

But we amateurs are not concerned with grafted queens as we can get our cells by simpler and probably better methods.

Starting is the word generally used when the bees build a cell around a larva on the comb in which the egg was laid without any transference by the bee-keeper.

Acceptance will be evident in about twelve to eighteen hours, for here we will have queenless and broodless bees who will have been given a number of selected grubs which are assumed to be of the right age, and they will clearly accept or reject in the first few hours.

Starting may well take a little longer, for in this case the bees will have larvæ of different ages from which to choose; in such a comb we may find some of the larvæ with an extra quantity of larval food before there is any sign of actual cell building. This excess of larval food is by no means always a sign that the bees are starting queen cells, for we will often see a surprising difference in the quantity of food in brood cells; nevertheless, I have seen it as evidence of what we might call acceptance.

We would use the expression " accepted " where we had given the bees a specially prepared comb in which we had selected the eggs or larvæ upon which we wished them to build cells, when they had started cells in accordance with our plans. It refers specifically to that short period of some hours during which the proffered larvæ are accepted or refused.

Stage 2 : Cell Building

This is the period of approximately five days from the hatching of the egg to the sealing of the cell, during which the bees feed the larva and build and complete the cell.

Bees must be starting in the Super before the operation

Brood chambers with Queen & brood in all stages

BEFORE

DEMAREE Before

The rest of the unsealed brood is now in this brood chamber

The Super acts as a barrier between the Queen and the unsealed brood thus increasing the urge to build cells

Queen with one frame of unsealed brood. All other frames must be of sealed brood or empty combs

AFTER

DEMAREE and after

DRONE TRAP. When fixed to the hive entrance bees can pass freely through the lower part of the excluder. Drones cannot pass excluder but come up through cone escapes and are trapped in the upper box. The hole in the cone escape is enlarged so as to pass a drone.

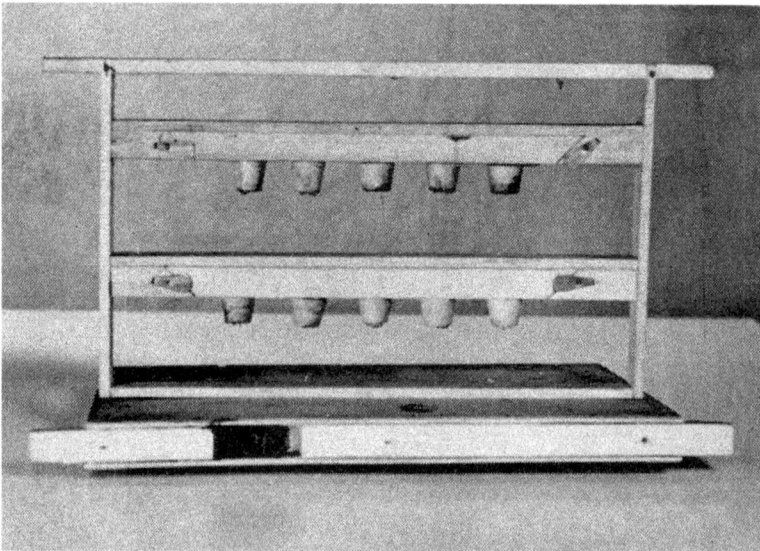

ABOVE; A FRAME FOR HOLDING CELL CUPS, normally used in the cell – building colony when grafting but also useful for the Barbeau or Alley method. BELOW; A DUMMY FEEDER is useful in mating nuclei as it is less likely to cause robbing. The bees enter through the hole in the side. It is filled through the hole in the top.

A most important period, remember, for it is the treatment of the larva during this period which decides whether it will emerge as a queen or just as a worker.

STAGE 3 : INCUBATION AND EMERGENCE

Incubation is the period between sealing and emergence when the cell only needs warmth and humidity. Cells can be incubated in incubators in the same way as hens' eggs, but the amateur will no doubt follow the old-fashioned method and let the bees do the work ; there is probably much to be said in its favour.

STAGE 4 : MATING

The mating stage is self explanatory, I might perhaps have coupled emergence with it, rather than with the incubation stage, for in our apiaries queens will usually emerge in mating nuclei, but I think mating is better considered separately.

As I have already said, amateurs will usually reduce these stages to two by combining the first and second, and having cells *started* and *built* in the same strong colony, and then transferring them to a weaker colony or nucleus for stages three and four : *emergence* and *mating*. The incubation period lasts about seven to eight days, and during this period the transfer from one stage to the other will be made. As there are several days to choose from, it is not difficult for the week-end bee-keeper to arrange his queen breeding programme to fit in with his spare time.

It may well be that as the amateur progresses and perhaps becomes a little more ambitious and wishes to breed a few more queens than he requires for his own use, he may well introduce an *acceptance* stage and have his larvæ accepted by queenless bees, his cells *built* and *incubated* in other colonies ; his queens finally *emerging* and *mating* in nuclei, thus introducing three separate stages ; but this is not always necessary, for a queen can pass through all the stages in one colony if that is desired.

Having briefly examined the four stages, we must remember that we are proposing to breed *good* queens. We want to breed them from parents of our own selection and at a time of our own choosing. Therefore it is necessary to try to understand the bees' requirements during each of these stages, so we must consider them in more detail.

Chapter V

WHEN BEES WILL START CELLS

BEES will start cells under one of three impulses : swarming, supersedure, or the emergency impulse of queenlessness.

As we are aiming to breed selectively I am afraid we cannot use the swarming impulse, for although it is Nature's way of propagating the species, and good queens are produced in this way, yet such queens are only good physically, and from the point of view of improving our strain we are just as likely to go backward as forward. All our knowledge of heredity goes to show that constant selection is necessary to maintain the strain, and Nature left to itself seems to go backward from the point of view of the selective breeder and to revert to the strain from which the improved stock was originally bred.

So we must reject swarming as a queen-breeding impulse, for apart from the fact that it tends to " breed in " swarming we have no control over the time of swarming, nor can we be sure that our selected queen will swarm, especially as we will breed from those who do not swarm excessively.

The thrill of a swarm is never lost even by the oldest of bee-keepers, annoying though it may be, and we can take a lesson from the swarm when we are breeding queens, in that the conditions in the hive at swarming time are usually ideal for queen breeding, plenty of bees, plenty of food, a growing strength—in fact a colony that is all on the up and up and in great heart, and that is why the queens are physically good. We will also find that the easiest time to raise queens is during the swarming season.

The Supersedure Impulse

Queens raised under the supersedure impulse, when the bees feel that they need a new queen, are also bred naturally and by Nature's methods, but natural supersedure is not under our control. It is, however, possible to induce what is assumed to be a supersedure impulse in the hive, and by doing this we can :

    (*a*) raise queens from our selected colony ;

    (*b*) at the time most suited to ourselves ;

    (*c*) without amplifying the swarming tendency ;

    (*d*) with very little interference with the work of the colony in getting honey.

This method is based on the fact that if the queen is excluded from a part of the hive where there is young brood the bees appear to behave as though the queen was failing, and will often, *but not always*, build cells. In a normal colony the queen is generally busy expanding the existing patch of brood. When we exclude her from it, it would seem that she might appear to be failing, and that is why this is believed to be a supersedure impulse.

It is quite a simple matter to produce these conditions although it needs a little forethought and planning.

We can either isolate the queen in a single brood chamber by using the conventional excluder above the frames, and with it using a vertical excluder cut to the shape of a division board and fitting the brood chamber exactly. The more popular way is to take the brood into an upper chamber above the excluder, as in the Demaree method of swarm control, which I will describe in a later chapter.

As a rule bees will not build cells under these conditions unless there is a real isolation between the confined queen and the unsealed brood. This is usually achieved by putting a barrier of honey between the two. To do this we can put a couple of combs of honey on either side of the excluder in the brood chamber, or use the supers in the case of the Demaree.

I have already said that bees will not always build cells under these conditions, but there is one further measure we can employ that will make the starting of cells as certain as anything is in bee-keeping and that is temporary confinement. This confinement seems to give a great urge to cell starting whatever method we may employ, and when used with the Demaree we only need a wooden frame covered with wire gauze or perforated zinc that we can put under the upper brood chamber. Its size will depend upon the style of brood chamber used.

Raising queens under this method has the advantages of simplicity, and of little interference with the colony; we cannot be sure that the bees will start cells, however, and this seems to be especially true of non-swarming strains and may also depend on the time of year.

Some experts say that queens bred in this way are not so good physically as those produced by other methods, yet there appears to be no reason why this should be so provided that sufficient thought is given to the needs of the bees at the critical times.

The Emergency Impulse (Queenlessness)

When rendered queenless, either by accident or design, bees are almost certain to start queen cells. They are generally started after about twelve hours of queenlessness, and under the sense of emergency the first cells may be started on larvæ which are too old, or by bees which are not yet ready to build cells. Subsequent cells will of course be started on larvæ of the right age.

To render a whole colony queenless will mean a considerable set-back in its season's work, but there is a simple alternative, and that is to use a relatively small number of bees in a swarm box to get the cells started, having them built and completed in a queen-right colony. At first sight this method may appear to be a little more troublesome. Nevertheless, it is the most certain way to get cells started and the only one to use if more than a small number of queens is required.

Chapter VI

THE ESSENTIALS OF CELL BUILDING

The Bees.

OUR cell building bees must be of the right age for this work, and that may be taken to mean nurse bees.

It has been said that old bees can build cells just as well as young bees ; it may be true, for perhaps old bees which have not produced larval food in the days of their youth can do so later in life. As we cannot enquire into the past life of our bees, we will choose those *relatively* young bees which normally do the nursing in the hive. Wedmore tells us that bees start to feed old larvæ on the third to sixth day of their lives, and proceed to feed young larvæ from the sixth day on. This is worth noting, for it would seem that the younger nurse bees may only be able to produce the lower grade of brood food which is fed to the older worker larvæ. Therefore we should look for our cell building bees in a strong colony where plenty of *young* larvæ are being fed, for it is on those combs we will find the best bees for our purpose.

Now it is also very important that the bees should be in the right condition to build cells at the time when the cells are started. If we are allowing the bees to choose their own larvæ, then it may be that they will get themselves into good cell building condition before they set to work ; at least, we can say we have given them the opportunity to do so.

If, however, we are using a method in which we select larvæ ourselves, then we must be sure that the building impulse shall have been created some time before the selected larvæ are given. If we are starting with queenless and brood-less bees, a waiting period is necessary, as during this period of waiting the bees will have been secreting large quantities of larval food and will be in fine condition. Alternatively, bees which have started cells already will make an excellent start on fresh larvæ if their own cells are removed, but such cells should be removed before they are too far advanced, for bees do not, as a rule, do so well with a second batch of cells if their own are nearly completed. It is important to use bees that have been rearing brood, as bees that have been without brood are not in good condition to start cells.

Food. Remember that food means not only honey, but also pollen and water. Honey is the carbohydrate that produces the heat and energy, but the bee is made of pollen; without it, you cannot make a bee, and it is pollen that contains the vitamins. The bees have to convert this honey and pollen into brood food and they cannot do that without water.

If we could be sure of having our cells built in a strong colony, and when there was a flow on, the bees would no doubt attend to their own requirements. As the flow is not very dependable in this country, and as we may be starting cells in hives where there are but few flying bees, we had better assume that the question of food is up to us.

Feeding should begin about four days before cells are started so as to get the bees into the right condition, and should be considered right through the cell building period so that there is always a surplus available. This surplus should be honey and pollen not sugar syrup.

Has it occurred to you that shortage of food in a hive at any time when brood rearing is in progress may well mean that the larvæ are actually undernourished? When we are raising queens the whole difference between the worker and the queen is decided by those precious five days of feeding— five vital days—there must never be a possibility of undernourishment.

We should remember the need for sufficient food in the colony of the breeder queen, for it is here that the feeding of our selected larvæ will start.

Larvæ of the Right Age.

The important thing here is that the larva must be *young enough* at the time that the bees start to feed it as a queen. Some experts like larvæ not more than twelve hours old, others say that those up to thirty-six hours old are just as good, and there are those who say the larvæ may be as much as three days old.

We must remember that in their consideration of the larval age, the grafters have to have larvæ that are old enough to stand the shock of being transferred from one cell to another in the grafting process; it may well be that as the older larvæ stand the change better than the younger ones, they do, in fact, produce equally good queens in the circumstances.

We are not going to attempt grafting, yet we may wish to breed queens by one of the methods in which we will select the larvæ ourselves, so it is as well that we should learn to recognise larvæ of different ages.

If we look at a comb in which the queen has recently been laying we shall see in more or less concentric circles eggs, larvæ of different ages, and sealed brood. The books tell us that the age of the egg may be recognised by its position in the cell, vertical to the cell base on the first day, at an angle of 45 degrees on the second day, and lying on the bottom of the cell on the last day before it hatches. Like most things in bee-keeping, this is not always true.

The amateur may be satisfied to have his queen cells built on the comb in which the egg was laid, and so let the bees do the choosing. We give them a comb with both eggs and newly hatched larvae, then whatever the experts may say, we know the bees have larvæ of the right age. We might then assume that as the bees had freedom of choice, they would naturally choose larvæ of the right age, but it appears that this is not always so ; they will sometimes, as though inspired by a sense of urgency or panic, start cells on larvæ which are in fact too old.

This warning is often repeated, yet I seldom find that my bees make this mistake. Perhaps one day we shall find out that they only do so in certain circumstances.

Of course we must guard against it by checking up on the date the cells are sealed; if a cell is sealed on the third day we are safe in assuming that the larva was more than thirty-six hours old, and such a cell should be cut out leaving the bees to complete those which are less advanced.

It may, however, be noted that some bees seal cells much earlier than others, having first put in all the royal jelly that will be required.

I feel sure that if the reader has grasped the essential points that I have discussed in this chapter, he will appreciate that by an examination of the cells on about the third day he will be able to recognise any doubtful ones, and cut out those that are sealed; he can then leave the bees to complete the others, feeling quite confident that they have been built under ideal conditions.

Chapter VII

STARTING CELLS WITH QUEENLESS BEES

W E have already mentioned that queenless bees are almost certain to start cells, and for this reason it is important that we should consider this method; it enables us to be sure of getting cells started when we want them. Our queen breeding season is a short one, and it can be very aggravating to find that the bees have failed to start the cells we need to fit in with our plans.

We can either use a queenless colony to start the cells and allow the same colony to complete them, or we can have them completed elsewhere. Alternatively, we can have the cells started by a relatively small number of bees, in which case the building and completing must be done in either a queenless colony or in a queen-right colony which has been previously prepared. Once cells have been started, it is not so difficult to get the bees to complete them.

Using a Queenless Colony.

There are two distinct ways of preparing a colony for cell starting :—

    (a) Removing the queen and all unsealed brood;

    (b) Removing the queen only, and waiting until all brood is sealed.

Let us consider both these methods.

The First Method.

The queen, and all unsealed brood is removed at one operation, the bees, especially the nurse bees which are feeding the brood, are shaken back into the hive, and the brood is given to other hives which are strong enough to take care of it.

After four or five hours, the selected eggs or larvæ are inserted. This method has much to commend it, for there will be plenty of bees to do the work, and the bees are flying freely, which is considered to be quite an important point for cell builders. The bees may be confined for a few hours before the larvæ are given to them.

The Second Method.

In this case only the queen is removed, when of course, the bees will build cells ; if we have used the breeder queen's colony, then of course the cells will have been built on our selected larvæ, and all we need do is to check up to make sure that the bees have not started too soon, on larvæ that was too old. We will get good queens by this method but there are a few snags—the bees will start the cells on existing larvæ, and in my experience they show remarkably little consideration for the bee-keeper who wishes to cut them out and distribute them to nuclei. Maybe it's just my luck, or just their cussedness, but I generally find these cells either built on wires or built in pairs in such a way as to make it very difficult to separate them.

If, however, we are using this method with a colony other than the breeder colony, it is necessary to wait nearly eight days until all the brood is sealed, and then cut out all the cells which have been built before introducing the selected larvæ. To be sure of finding all the cells, the combs must be shaken free from bees. There is no queen to be injured, and as we propose to destroy the cells shaking will do no harm. We should never shake a comb with good cells which we wish to keep, nor, of course, one with a queen in full lay.

Theoretically, this is a good method. The bees have no larvæ of their own, and the nurse bees are already building cells, and so will be full of the necessary brood food, so the selected larvæ can be inserted right away.

Recently, a German expert (Gontarski) raises a doubt about this, for he contends that the normal conditions for raising good queens are not present in a hive that has been queenless for some time. He advises caging the queen at the start so that she cannot lay in all the combs, then she is removed only one day before the new larvæ are given. I have no experience of this method, but we do know that bees will not keep on continually building fresh batches of cells; this may well indicate some falling-off of their cell building ability. I would assume that a Whyte cage, one that takes the whole comb, would be a suitable cage for this method.

Remember that when either of these methods is adopted the colony must be fed for a few days before, as well as during, the operation. A single colony must not be allowed to build too many cells, but as a guide ten or twelve will not be too many for a good ten-frame colony.

In a Swarm Box

Whilst this method may appear to be a little more troublesome, it is the most certain way to get cells started, as it makes use of that additional urge created by confinement. Only a small number of bees are used and these are only required for twenty-four hours, so that they may be borrowed from a colony without much interference with its normal life.

The cells so started can be completed in the upper half of a queen-right colony which has been properly prepared, and this colony, too, is not affected in its work.

The young bees from four or five frames are shaken into a prepared swarm box and confined with ample ventilation for about five hours in a queenless state.

The best type of swarm box to use is one about half the size of a brood chamber that will take about five combs, the whole of the bottom being covered with wire gauze to allow good ventilation without too much light. The lid is best arranged with a slot in the centre through which the comb of selected larvæ can be inserted without removing the whole of the lid.

Bees in confinement generate a lot of heat and will be less restless if confined in darkness. Into the box put two combs with plenty of honey and pollen, leaving a space in the centre for our selected larvæ. Remembering the bees' need for water (they cannot consume the honey undiluted, and they cannot fly to get water) we can either

> (*a*) fill the empty cells in the combs with water by dropping it on to them;
>
> (*b*) provide a dummy feeder with water in it; or
>
> (*c*) simply feed with very thin syrup.

When all is prepared, go to a colony when the old bees are flying and shake the young bees off four or five frames into the swarm box. Close the box and keep it in a cool, shady place for four or five hours, then introduce the selected larvæ.

Next day the cells will have been started, or, as we should more correctly say, the larvæ will have been accepted, and they should be removed to a stronger colony which has been properly prepared for cell building, as the swarm box will not be strong enough to complete all the cells. However, a small number may be completed in the swarm box, provided that food supplies are maintained, and that the bees are allowed to fly normally. A cast or swarm headed by a virgin will build good cells if the queen is removed two days after hiving and eggs or larvæ are given.

Chapter VIII

THE SUPERSEDURE IMPULSE

USING A DEMAREE FOR STARTING OR BUILDING CELLS

WE have already seen that when the queen is excluded from a part of the hive and brood is present in the excluded part, the bees appear to assume that the queen is failing and cells are often started. Now whilst the bees will not always start cells under these conditions, they can generally be relied on to complete cells that have once been started, so that such a colony offers an ideal cell-building colony for cells which have been started in a swarm box or in some other way.

The simple way to arrange this is to carry out the manipulation commonly called a "Demaree," which is used as a method of swarm control, and can be quite effective. It can be used in queen production with no real interference with the work of the colony.

HOW TO DEMAREE

In the early spring the colony is built up by feeding if necessary until it occupies two brood chambers, a super is added over an excluder, and by about the end of May, except in late districts, the bees should at least be starting in the super. (Many bee-keepers try to carry out this manipulation before the bees are really strong enough, and it is important to have the bees occupying the twenty combs before we commence the operation.) Then stand the two brood chambers aside, and put an empty one on the floor of the hive. Go through the combs, find the queen and place the comb on which she is found in the new brood chamber. Go through the remaining combs and put all the empty ones or those with only sealed and emerging brood in with

34

the queen.   All those with unsealed brood (except the one on which the queen was found) are put in a second brood chamber.   The queen excluder is put over the new brood chamber with the queen in it, then over that the super, and finally the chamber with the unsealed brood.   The queen, therefore, has no access to the young brood, and this creates a cell-building impulse which is generally assumed to be the supersedure impulse.   This colony will now make an excellent cell-building colony for cells started elsewhere, but we will now consider the question of getting cells started in a Demareed stock if it is desired to do so.

Starting Cells in a Demareed Colony

Although this may be a good way of getting cells it is not very reliable.   Some strains seem reluctant to build cells, and it is therefore advisable to intensify the cell-building impulse by a temporary confinement of the bees in the upper brood chamber.

This is done twenty-four hours after the first manipulation when most of the nurse bees will be in the upper chamber and most of the older bees will be below.   A screen board of wire gauze is inserted below the upper chamber for twenty-four hours and at the end of this period it must be removed.

In starting cells by this method, we must remember all the essentials I have outlined and we can use the colony of the breeder queen, in which case the cells will be built on her larvæ.   The bees may be allowed to complete these cells after we have checked up to see that none were started on old larvæ and nuclei can be made up from the combs themselves. One snag in this is that the cells so built may be all on the one comb, and it is often difficult to cut them out for transfer to other nuclei.   It may help if we select the larvæ ourselves by slightly opening the mouths of the cells, being careful to avoid disturbing the larva as we do so.   Let me just summarise this simple method.

In the Breeder's Colony.

(1) feed half-a-pint of syrup daily for four days ; then
(2) Demaree, and after twenty-four hours
(3) insert screen for twenty-four hours ;
(4) check quality of cells after three days ;
(5) remove cells after sealing and before emergence.

In Another Colony.

In this case we must carry out the Demaree seven days before we wish to insert the selected larvæ, and cut out the cells started by the bees on their own larvæ immediately before the new grubs are inserted, so the procedure is :—

(1) feed half-a-pint of syrup daily for four days ; then
(2) Demaree, and after seven days ;
(3) cut out cells on existing brood, insert screen and selected larvæ ;
(4) remove screen after twenty-four hours ;
(5) remove cells after sealing, but before emergence.

We may notice that in this method the bees are not queen-less ; presumably the objections to a second batch of cells do not apply. In fact if a good stock once starts cells in this way it will often continue to build further batches if fresh larvæ is given as each batch is removed.

A word of warning. Take especial care to see that you do not allow a virgin to emerge in the top chamber. If you do your other cells will be destroyed and the virgin may squeeze through the excluder and kill the old queen. Needless to say the virgin trapped above the excluder cannot fly to mate, and it is often said that such virgins become drone layers. I am told, however, that very often they just disappear without laying at all.

Chapter IX

HOW TO GET THE LARVÆ

WE can get the larvæ merely by choosing a frame of brood containing eggs and larvæ of all ages and by leaving the bees to build cells where they will. If we do it in this way we will probably find many of the cells built in awkward places, even on the wires, and thus difficult to cut out when we wish to distribute them to nuclei. There is, however, another point, the bees cannot build cells properly on old combs, for it appears that they are unable to tear down an old cell with its tough walls when it is occupied by a larva, even though they often tear down empty cells.

It is better, therefore, to use newly built comb for queen breeding, and the best way to get this is to prepare a frame with a " starter "—a strip of foundation about three inches wide. This is inserted in the breeder's hive about a week before the larvæ will be required, so that the bees may build the comb and the queen may lay eggs in it. To ensure that the bees do this we insert it in the centre of the brood nest, and keep a feeder on the hive, but we must always see that there is not too much room for the queen to lay elsewhere in the hive. If the hive is sufficiently crowded the bees will draw the foundation out on the first day and the queen will lay on the second day, so that we may find newly hatched larvæ on the sixth day in the upper part of the comb they have built, whilst the lower part will be filled with eggs.

Next, this lower edge is trimmed away so that the newly hatched larvæ are on the lower edge ; we select these at intervals, and slightly open the mouths of the cells where we wish queen cells to be built, destroying the larvæ in the intervening cells. Thus we get cells built evenly spaced and easy to transfer to our nuclei.

When handling combs with larvæ, care must be taken to avoid chilling the brood, or exposing it to bright sunlight, which by its strong ultra violet rays can be more harmful to young larvæ than actual low temperature.

It is often said that the work is best done indoors, and at a temperature of not less than 75 degrees F., but it may be equally important to remember that whilst we are doing this little job the larvæ are not receiving that vital attention from the nurse bees, so don't worry too much about the temperature if it means prolonging the time the brood is away from its attendants.

Other Methods.

MILLER. This is the same as the method I have given above, except that triangular-shaped starters are used. If taken at the right time these will offer more exposed edges, and thus we can get a greater number of cells.

ALLEY. In this method a diagonal strip is cut from the comb in which the larvæ are found. After the larvæ on the back face have been destroyed, it is fastened with a little hot wax to a bar in a frame, then the larvæ can be selected as in the first method.

BARBEAU. The original idea was to use a simple punch, just a piece of 3/8 tube sharpened on the edge, and with it to cut out the cell required and mount it in a special holder, but other experts have introduced modifications of this method and any of them may well commend itself to the amateur. Snelgrove suggests a modification of it, using a larger punch with a sliding square-ended tube within it. When the larva has been punched out in the large tube, the smaller tube is used to push it back again, so that it may be fixed with heated wax to a wooden cell holder, or other suitable base.

STANLEY'S PATENT uses a cell holder and cutter combined, the cutter having a plastic tip. The cell is built upon the actual plastic tip so as to avoid risk of chilling the larvæ by contact with a metal cutter. It offers a very simple way of selecting individual larvæ.

When selecting larvæ by these methods we should not only look for those that are newly hatched, but we should also see that they have a good supply of larval food.

If we examine a comb of unsealed larvæ we will generally see that some have more food than others ; these are the ones to choose. It is also important to choose larvæ all of the same age, as the bees appear to reject more grubs when there is a considerable difference in their ages.

We can, by another modification of the Barbeau method, let the bees make their own selection. Two empty frames are laid on top of the combs in the cell starting colony, and on top of these the comb of larvæ is laid face downwards. All is covered up, and after a couple of days, the bees will have started cells which can be cut out and fixed to cell holders for completion in a cell building colony.

Before this method is attempted it is wise to devise some means of covering the combs, for a frame laid flat will not fit into a standard shallow chamber.

Chapter X

EMERGENCE

AFTER sealing, the cells merely require keeping at the proper temperature until the virgins emerge. Large breeders often use incubators and find them satisfactory.

It may well be that the humidity of the hive and the companionship of the bees is to be desired during the period of incubation, so the amateur will probably prefer to leave them in the cell-building colony. If this is done it is essential to see that the virgins are not allowed to emerge unless each cell has been properly caged, and I do not advise the amateur to do this until he has gained some experience.

It is therefore better to transfer the cells to nuclei before the queens emerge, and experience goes to show that the sooner this is done the better, provided that the nuclei are strong enough to care for them and that the larva has had time to open her cocoon, e.g., one day after the cell is sealed. If the cells are introduced when on the point of emergence, there is a greater risk of the virgin being killed.

The actual date of emergence is governed not only by the age of the larva on which the cell was started, but to some extent by the feeding during the cell-building process and the temperature during incubation; hence a cell started on thirty-six-hour-old larva might be ready to emerge in eleven or twelve days after acceptance, or seven days after sealing.

We must learn to recognise a " ripe " cell, that is, one that is nearly ready to emerge. Look at a cell when it is first built and you will see that the point is thick and looks very much like the body of the cell. As it becomes " ripe," the bees thin it down at the tip, this thinner, roughened surface is quite unmistakable once it has been noted. It is usually darker in colour than the body of the cell.

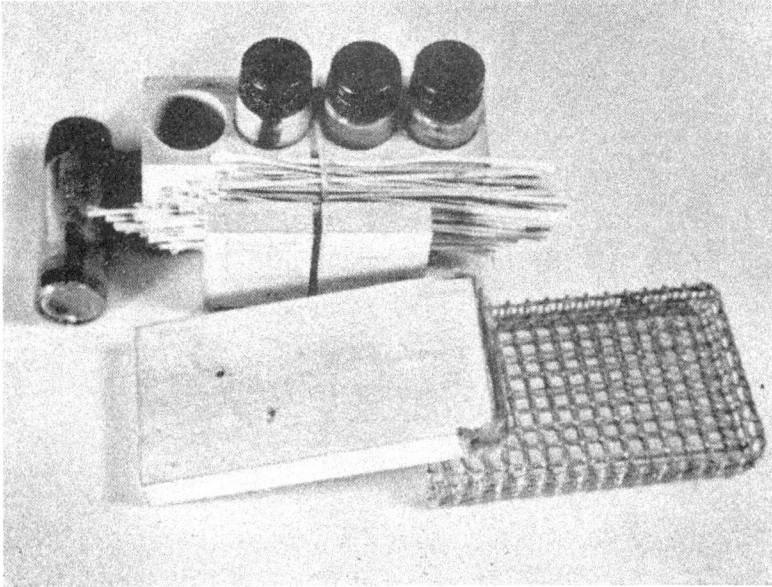

QUEEN MARKING OUTFIT. The cage is slipped over the queen, and when she runs up, the wooden follower which is tipped with plush is used to hold her at the top. A dab of paint is applied with one of the spills – any quick – drying cellulose is suitable.

EXAMINING A NUCLEUS. Note the dummy feeder and the quilt tacked to the centre board to avoid the risk of queens running into the adjoining nucleus.

THE AUTHOR'S MATING HIVES. Made half the size of National hives and with half – size crown boards. Ordinary National roofs are used. Those illustrated have strips of wood tacked inside to allow for feeders. These can be placed on hives when uniting.

MATING HIVE FOR FOUR NUCLEI. The entrances are placed one on each side and one on the each end, so that flying queens are less likely to enter the wrong nucleus.

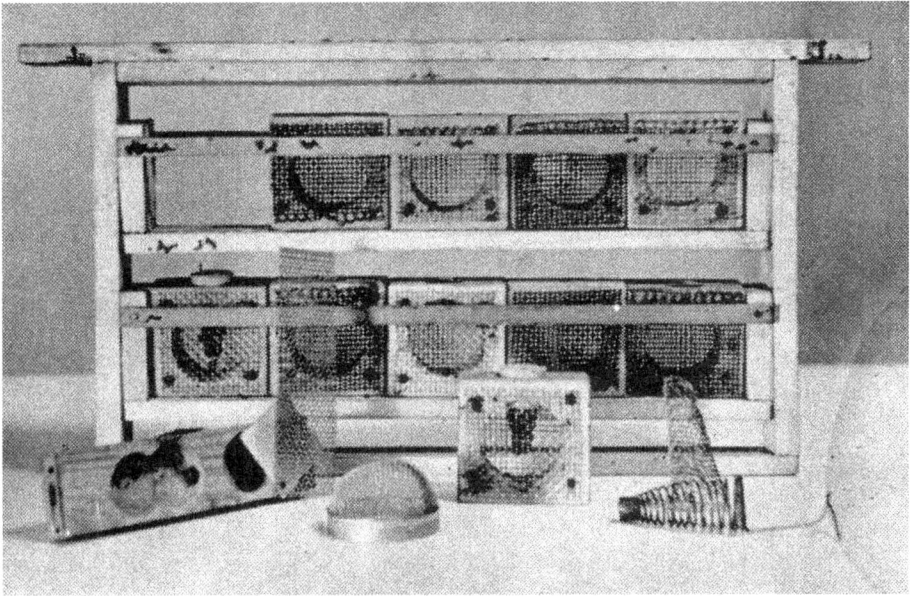

CAGES OF VARIOUS KINDS. Bottom left, a good travelling cage. It is coated with wax and there is a waxed paper to cover the candy hole – both preventing absorption of moisture from candy. Also pipe cover cage, cell cages and virgin cages with frame.

A GOOD INTRODUCING CAGE – an improvement on the Jay Smith cage. There are two entrances to the cage, one of which is covered with excluder. This is a good cage for cells, the virgin can be given access to natural stores and can be released without undue disturbance.

It is better for the beginner to arrange for his queens to emerge in nuclei, but as his skill improves, he may wish to use some cages. Caged virgins deteriorate very rapidly, and are much more difficult to introduce as they become older; therefore caging should not be attempted until some experience has been gained.

Cages are especially useful where mating nuclei are held up by bad weather, and we have a fresh batch of cells nearing emergence; again, there is some saving of time in the mating nuclei if virgins are introduced instead of cells.

It is most important to see that virgins kept in cages should have access to food, both honey and pollen for choice, as although bees will feed a caged queen, they do not seem to feed virgins, it is better therefore to cage on a comb.

One method of caging virgins is to use a cage made of excluder zinc, which holds a complete comb. Combs with cells are placed in these in the top box of a Demareed stock, where the virgins are allowed to emerge, the virgin then having the run of a comb with stores in it. Although there would appear to be some danger of virgins getting through the excluder, I am assured by those who have used these cages that this seldom happens. A virgin emerging under these conditions is not really caged, and would suffer in no way from confinement, and such a virgin introduced to a nuclei would mate very quickly. Always be careful when caging virgins or handling them to see they don't fly.

Chapter XI

QUEEN MATING NUCLEI

THREE British Standard combs (one of stores and two of brood) make a very good mating nucleus. Most of the brood should be nearly emerging ; there are many good reasons. The emerging bees will strengthen the nucleus and it may be that this increase in the number of young bees stimulates the bees' urge for a fertile queen, and thus helps to get the virgins mated. It is thought that unsealed brood in the hive delays mating. I do not know that this is true, but if there is much of it there may not be enough bees to care for it properly.

Old bees are much more likely to accompany the queen when she flies and so give us a mating swarm.

Food supplies must be maintained, for there will be but few working bees, and a slow feed at mating time will stimulate the desire to mate.

So much for the nucleus ; but what can we do to help the queen herself ? Entrances should be free from obstruction, but protected from cross winds which will make landing more difficult. They should be easily identifiable so as to minimise the risk of the virgin entering the wrong hive. The line of flight should be arranged so that it is not the same as that of the main colonies, otherwise a nervous virgin may well " follow the crowd " into one of the hives.

Virgins *may* fly two days after emergence, and *may* mate three days after that, but expert opinions vary as to the most *probable* date which is generally from the seventh to the twelfth day. These earlier matings are not common, and it may be that they only occur when the virgin has been confined in her cell by the bees, as she sometimes is.

The queen commences to lay about two days after she has

mated. She may at first lay a few drone eggs, but I am told that queens that do this do not as a rule turn out to be very good queens.

With a little experience it is easy to judge when a virgin has mated, for her abdomen begins to fill out and there seems to be a general change in her demeanour, but she must not be removed until we have definite evidence that the mating has been satisfactory. The first sign will be an evenly laid patch of eggs, or young larvæ, but we must wait until the brood is sealed before we can be quite sure. The more experienced who wish to mate several batches of virgins may decide that they cannot wait long enough for the brood to be sealed, and again may wish to avoid allowing the nuclei to become too strong when there would be more risk of mating swarms; nevertheless, I would advise the beginner to wait. Don't inspect your nuclei too soon or too often, and never between 11 a.m. and 4 p.m. on days when the virgin is likely to be flying. I have lost too many good queens through being too anxious to have a look. Leave your nuclei alone, except for food, until twelve days have elapsed after the date on which emergence is expected; sometimes you may find too much brood, but in the long run you will save a lot of queens.

We used to think that queens mated once only, but there is plenty of evidence to-day that they sometimes mate more than once. This dual mating only occurs during the mating period, for it is generally recognised that a virgin must mate within about twenty-eight days, otherwise she cannot mate at all.

I would assume that if there is a second mating it will occur before the queen starts to lay. Whether both matings are effective is not known, but it has been suggested that only when the first mating has not been effective does the queen mate a second time. If it is established that queens do have more than one effective mating, then some variations in the progeny of such queens might well be expected. Whatever the facts may be about double matings, all we need say here is that there is no need to worry if you see a queen flying a day or so after you had assumed she was mated.

Making Nuclei

One of the most common troubles when making nuclei is that too many bees return to the parent hive ; this is, of course, avoided when they can be removed to other apiaries, but the amateur will normally have to keep them at home. Some experts keep the nuclei confined for three days in a cool dark place, in order to overcome this trouble ; others say that the entrance should be stuffed with grass, which the bees will remove. In practice I don't do any of these things. I rely on a little judgment and common sense. If we make up a nucleus on a good flying day, most of the flying bees will be out and we shall get a high proportion of young bees. That fine old American expert Miller tells us that nuclei made from queenless bees give less trouble in this way.

As already mentioned, I suggest three standard frames, two frames of sealed brood well covered with young bees, and one frame of stores, will constitute your nucleus, but shake the young bees off some other frames which will make up for any loss of flying bees.

Shallow combs can be used for nuclei and are more economical in bees ; these are especially convenient for bee-keepers who winter their colonies with a super of shallow frames above, as an extension to the brood chamber. It may be no harm to digress here and say how valuable this method of management is as a means of giving the colony adequate winter stores in districts where there is no late flow and where only a ten-comb British Standard brood chamber is used.

In making up a nucleus from a colony other than the colony of the selected queen, we will have to avoid the strange drones. This is easily done by filtering the bees through a queen excluder. A queen excluder is placed over the colony from which the bees are being taken, and above that an empty

44

brood chamber, in which the combs of brood are placed after a shake to clear them of bees. In a very short time the brood will be covered with bees which will come up through the excluder, and the selected drones can be added afterwards as drones are readily accepted by any colony whether strange or otherwise.

Don't forget that if there is drone brood in the combs, there will be strange drones later on. It is best to be hard hearted and kill such brood by slicing the tops off the cells. Drones wander, so it is unlikely that you will keep your nuclei free from strangers, but the more care you take the better your chances of a pure mating.

When working from a Demareed colony where a cell has been built on an original comb, this comb and one other, with a third frame of stores, makes an excellent nucleus complete with cells, and is perhaps the simplest of all methods.

In deciding when to make a nucleus it will be well to consider the exact purpose for which it is to be used, and whether the cells will be caged or not. These points, however, will be dealt with in the paragraph on inserting cells.

Managing Nuclei

Nuclei generally require feeding, as they contain but few foraging bees, and really great care is needed to guard against robbing; entrances must therefore be small. I prefer to use soft candy for feeding as it causes less excitement and there is of course no spilling of syrup, which can easily start robbing. One expert I know uses soft brown sugar which he tips into the hive; it contains more moisture than white sugar, and as it is not being used for winter stores, does no harm to the bees. If, however, syrup is used, it is best to feed from a dummy feeder within the hive, and to fill this in the evenings only.

If the queens are left for about six days after they commence laying, this will generally keep the nucleus strong enough, but of course, the time will depend on the period which has elapsed since the last queen was laying so a little judgment must be used.

Some of my less experienced readers may find it useful to know that in the general handling of nuclei it is not necessary to follow all the text book rules about uniting. Small lots of young bees don't fight much, and if in transferring combs from one nucleus to another we give them a bit of an airing, we can swap odd combs of bees between one nucleus and another with impunity.

Inserting Cells in Nuclei

Some little judgment is required in deciding when nuclei will accept cells; we can be guided by the conditions in the nucleus in much the same way as we consider the conditions of a hive in which we wish to introduce a queen.

Nuclei which have started cells will easily accept other cells when their own are destroyed, especially when their own are sealed, or ready for sealing, but there is always a risk in giving ripe cells from which the virgin is due to emerge as such virgins are often killed.

Cells may be accepted as soon as the nucleus is aware of its queenlessness, say in two to twenty-four hours, and cells are nearly always accepted during this period if the bees have no brood of their own on which to raise cells.

Where there is young brood it is wise to cage the cell or if we can wait three days and then cut out the cells which have been started, introduction will be safer. In every case where a cell has been inserted in a nucleus when young brood is present, it is advisable to go through the nucleus a week later in case the bees have built cells of their own; any such cells should be destroyed as the bees may kill the virgin when she emerges, and retain one of their own choosing.

Feeding seems to help in getting cells accepted, especially later in the season. Bees seem to do most things better when the " flow is on," and we can simulate the flow by feeding in most of our queen-breeding operations.

Nuclei should not be over-fed to the point where they become blocked with stores.

We might summarise by saying that cells are most readily accepted if the nucleus :—

(1) has been queenless for twelve hours ;

(2) is being fed ;

(3) contains no young larvæ ;

(4) is made up three or four days before required or has started cells which can be destroyed ;

(5) when the cell is caged.

Cells should always be inserted in the warmest part of the nucleus hive, *i.e.*, near the top and in the centre, for although in nature the bees generally build their cells on the edges of the combs, in a nucleus there is some risk that if the weather turns cold the bees will cluster and the cell may be chilled. A cell with plenty of comb attached can be pinned through the wax part with a long pin, gripped between the top bars of two frames, or just pushed gently into the soft comb where it will stick.

Cages are easy to make, and it is well to have one or two handy, either a piece of gauze or a spiral of wire, conical shape, with an opening at the bottom about the size of a lead pencil, through which the tip of the cell can project and the occupant emerge. A plug such as a cork or piece of tin is needed in the top of the cage to prevent the bees from eating away the base of the cell ; the bees seem to attack queen cells at the base or sides when they want to destroy them, but never at the tip, presumably because of the cocoon.

NUCLEI FOR VIRGINS

Nuclei which are required for virgin queens can easily be made by shaking the bees from three combs and confining them for about four hours with *no unsealed brood* ; a virgin may then be run in and will usually be accepted without trouble.

This can be done in a swarm box and after introduction the bees can be hived as a swarm.

If the swarm box be covered with a piece of scrim or canvas, by poking a hole in the cover with a lead pencil, the virgin can be run in, or, if the bees are jolted to the bottom of the box the lid can be lifted and the queen dropped in amongst the bees.

Some experts wet the bees well with warm water and drop the virgin in straight away, which seems drastic to me, but is no doubt quite effective.

I may mention here that newly emerged virgins are readily accepted in almost any hive. It sometimes happens that we find cells from which the virgin has just started to emerge, in such a case we can open the cell and run the virgin in to any nucleus that requires one.

Chapter XII

GENERAL ADVICE

EQUIPMENT

NOT very much is required in the way of equipment by the small breeder. Nucleus hives will be required and of these there are many varieties. An ordinary brood chamber can be used, or if divided with tight-fitting division boards it can house two nuclei. Don't try to get three in, as you do need to be able to accommodate four combs in each nucleus at times.

My own fancy is to have brood chambers just half the size of my National hives (measured on the outside). Thus I have two boxes which, placed side by side, will take an ordinary roof: these can be placed together on top of a colony for uniting or over a screen board for warmth. The floors are flat with wooden strips half-an-inch thick tacked round the sides with two gaps for entrances on different sides and a strip down the centre where the two boxes meet, or entrances can be provided by boring a small hole in the end of the box itself.

I use half-size crown boards on them or half-quilts which I fix with drawing pins to the centre so as to ensure that the two queens do not meet. A few cell cages and some travelling queen cages, too, are desirable, as you are sure to find someone wanting a spare queen. Some method of marking queens is perhaps desirable so that we can see that a particular queen which we have recorded has not been superseded. Clipping the queen's wings will do this, but if I want to mark mine I use a spot of quick-drying cellulose enamel applied with a very thin piece of split cane, rather like one of the hairs from the domestic hard broom. There are many ways of holding the queen for marking, and one good method is to use a rim of card, the rim of the lid of a cardboard pill box, cover this with a piece of coarse net, pop it over the queen on the comb, and hold her whilst you dab her with the paint, wait a few seconds and then let her go.

WHEN TO START

In this country queens cannot usually be mated earlier than the middle of May or later than the middle of September. It is therefore wise not to start before late April or early May, except that, of course, some preliminary work may be done in building up colonies for cell building and production of selected drones, by giving drone comb if necessary to the breeder colony.

June and July are the best months for weather, so the beginner is advised to aim at getting his first queens in these months.

If, however, an earlier start is made it is necessary to be sure that suitable drones will be available.

This means that drones must be almost emerging before we can have queen cells started, so that if young drones can be seen in the hive we would be on the safe side.

KEEPING RECORDS

My own method of recording is to give each queen a number, of which the first two figures are the year and the others the number of the queen herself. I prefix this with a letter indicating the breeder, so in this way B4612 would be the twelfth queen bred in 1946, and her mother was " B." I give each breeder a letter and keep a note of her original number and parentage.

I also keep a kind of diary which shows what has to be done at different dates. As an appendix I have added a chart, and if the intending queen breeder will insert the actual date where I have put the day of rotation he will avoid missing any of the essential points. Needless to say, he should only use those columns which are applicable to the method he proposes to adopt, or modify the dates to suit some other plan he may wish to try. Others may have better memories than mine, but I find a chart of this sort indispensable.

Chapter XIII

TAKING CARE OF THE BREEDER QUEEN
AND SELECTING HER SUCCESSOR

HAVING selected our breeder queen because of the qualities of her offspring, and also because she is able to reproduce her own good qualities in her daughter queens, we have two things to consider.

Firstly, we must prolong her life as much as possible ; and secondly, we must think about the need for a successor when she passes on, for as a rule our breeder will not be a young queen herself.

The life of a bee, worker or queen, is not strictly measurable in terms of time, but rather in terms of work ; in other words, she just wears herself out.

The way to prolong her life, therefore, is to keep her in a small colony so that she cannot lay too many eggs ; a good prolific queen who has built up a big colony for two seasons has not much more egg laying left in her, and it is most likely that it is such a queen that we will choose as our first breeder. There is, however, one important point to note here, and that is that as we shall be breeding from her larvæ it is important that these larvæ shall have been well tended from birth ; so we must see to it that there are always plenty of young bees of the brood-food-secreting age in the hive, and, of course, adequate stores are necessary, too.

The death of a breeder queen is a sad occasion, for you form quite an affection for them. I know some commercial breeders do, and I expect it is true of them all ; nevertheless, it must come some day, so it is necessary to decide who is to take her place in due time. It is a good plan, therefore, to have a careful look at the work of one or two of her likely daughters after they have become established, so that we can see what their progeny are like.

I may be wrong, but I always feel that bees have a personality that one can recognise. Colour, appearance, and behaviour are all guides as to the continuity of a strain so that when you are handling a frame of the new queen's progeny, and watching the general work of the hive, you can sense if they are in fact the strain of bees you are trying to breed. Having decided that the daughter queen or queens appear to be satisfactory, breed one or two queens from *them* so that there are three generations in the apiary at the same time, then being satisfied with the qualities of the grand-daughter we can decide upon the mother as our next breeder queen.

SUBSEQUENT SELECTIONS

In order that we may improve the strain of our bees, it is necessary constantly to select breeders which show this ability to pass on the qualities we want. It is probably equally necessary to keep " culling " or eliminating those which have the qualities we do not want, for if we retain in our apiaries bees with undesirable qualities, we increase the risk of matings with their drones and in this way can have these undesirable qualities passed on.

When it is not possible to remove undesirable colonies from the apiary, then it is advisable to trap the drones from these colonies. These can be trapped by putting an excluder under the brood chamber to prevent them flying, but I think perhaps a proper drone trap fixed over the entrance in which the drones can be killed at the end of the day, is less cruel than the excluder; moreover, when an excluder is used, many drones will fly out when the colony is examined.

The process of selection must go on continuously, for although many children take after their parents, we keep on finding the ones that do not.

It might be that if we could find a pure-bred animal or insect, and mate it with an equally pure mate, the progeny would be pure, and in fact the laws of genetics would indicate that this is so, but there is no such creature, and so we must constantly cull and select.

By this process of constant selection we will in time produce a much purer strain and our queens will show less and less variation as time goes on. But there is another point here, and this is it, that having bred from a good queen, even our mis-mated queens are quite likely to give us excellent results in our working colonies for it is said that hybrids such as crosses between Italians and Blacks are often better workers than their parents.

This fact leads me to repeat again the need for selection for breeder qualities only, so don't always assume that the best worker is necessarily the best breeder.

Age in a breeder queen does not seem to affect her progeny, so we need not feel that a breeder is too old for her job.

The possibility of dual mating should be borne in mind as in such a case we could have the same queen producing two strains of bee. It is just a point to bear in mind when thinking of selection.

I hope I have not made this question of selection sound difficult for it is one of the fascinating parts of queen breeding. It is often very much a matter of guess, or " having a hunch " if you like, but it is well to understand what we are trying to do, for so long as we aim in the right direction, we are bound to improve our stock.

Chapter XIV

QUEEN INTRODUCTION

THERE are many excellent writings on this subject but for the sake of completeness I am adding a chapter on the methods which may be most useful for the amateur breeder. He will be mostly concerned with easy introduction in the apiary in which the queens are bred, as distinct from the introduction of queens which have travelled some distance.

Some of my readers may still rely on one of the older bee manuals for their guidance. In some of these books it is suggested that the scent of a strange queen is the cause of her rejection, but this theory is completely exploded. It seems much more likely that the behaviour of the queen herself and the state of the bees to whom she is to be introduced are big factors in successful acceptance.

It is quite possible to secure a fair percentage of satisfactory introductions by carefully following one method like a set of rules, but a breeder who will often want to introduce a queen quickly must have some knowledge of the conditions which are most favourable for acceptance.

Before we discuss these conditions, let us remember that we know practically nothing about a bee's emotions, what it feels, sees or hears, we have in fact no evidence that a bee hears at all, nor, of course, have we any evidence that it thinks ; so practically the whole of our knowledge is confined to the bee's reactions. In other words, we may know what the bee does under certain conditions, but we do not know why it does so, hence we need to be careful in giving a reason as to why the bees react in this way or that. No doubt the scent theory arose through jumping to a wrong conclusion, and this mistaken reason has been given over and over again in bee literature.

A queen can sometimes be introduced simply by picking the old laying queen off the comb and putting the new queen on in the same place. This is most likely to succeed when there is a flow on, and the new queen must be in the same condition as the old one, that is to say, a laying queen. So perhaps we may say that one of the ways to introduce a queen is when the bees don't know that you are doing it, for it really seems as though they don't.

But notice three points about this method—firstly, there is a flow on, food again, you see ; secondly, the queens are in similar condition, and thirdly, as most of the old bees are out foraging the queen is introduced to young bees. These conditions are always conducive to easy introduction, and there are some other points that are worth remembering, for example, a newly emerged virgin is readily accepted by any colony, even with a laying queen, and without any fuss or preparation, but after about the third day a virgin is most difficult to introduce. It may be that the newly emerged virgin is humble and hungry, very much like any other young bee, but at three days old she is a bright young thing running about the hive and perhaps spoiling for a fight.

Bees without a queen and without brood will generally accept anything, a laying queen, a virgin or a queen cell just as soon as they are aware of their loss, but a little later, when laying workers have started, introduction is almost impossible.

Never attempt to introduce queens if there is any robbing about and if you can choose your dates you will find October the best month. May is good but July and August are the most difficult periods.

Most of us have seen how the bees behave when they are suddenly deprived of their queen ; they appear to be in great distress, although again I say we do not know that this is so. We do know that the bees are much more willing to accept a new queen when this apparent distress is at its height, but that a little later, when they have presumably made preparations for cell building, queen introduction is most difficult.

So it seems that we must aim at having our bees in the right condition to meet the queen, and the queen in the right condition for the bees. It takes two to make a quarrel, or so my father used to say when my brother and I had a row, then he would bang our heads together as a kind of rough justice.

There seems to be a good deal of common sense in the ways bees behave, too, for some of the rules they obey are quite logical; bees with a virgin will readily accept a laying queen—well, they must be expecting a laying queen, mustn't they? But on the other hand, it's by no means easy to replace a laying queen with a virgin, other than one newly emerged which may pass unnoticed by the bees.

Then again, bees with sealed cells will accept another sealed cell, or a virgin; those with unsealed cells accept other unsealed cells, and if they have cells ready for sealing they will not normally reject sealed cells; all of which seems just common sense to me, and I think that if we carry this picture in our mind, we shall find queen introduction is not too difficult.

No method is infallible and no one method is better than any other in all circumstances. I often use the direct exchange when I think conditions are favourable, but I don't advise others to use it. It probably requires better judgment than we possess, so I will describe some of the methods I find most useful.

The Starvation Method

If we remove the queen from a hive the bees soon show evidence of their distress at her loss. This distress seems to increase and probably reaches its peak after about six hours; however, after about twelve hours they appear to have given up hope of her return, and commence cells so it would seem that after about six hours we have a colony earnestly desiring a queen, whereas after about twelve hours, the same colony, having decided to raise a new queen, will be less ready to accept any other.

Consequently, six hours after the colony has been made queenless we offer them a laying queen, similar to the one they lost and, if she behaves herself, they are generally eager to accept her. Queens are often aggressive, but if we take the queen we propose to introduce and keep her in a match box alone for half-an-hour with no food, we shall have a humble queen who only wants a home, food, and some bees to care for her. Then if we go to the colony and quietly lift a corner of the quilt or open the hole in the crown board, give a puff of smoke to drive the bees down momentarily, open our match box and let the queen run in, the bees will generally accept her. Whilst in the match box keep her warm, and the waistcoat pocket is a good place. With small lots of bees it is not necessary to wait six hours, two hours may be quite enough if conditions otherwise are favourable.

Re-queening with a Nucleus

I like this method. Go to the hive while the bees are flying ; find the queen and remove the frame she is on and two other frames—in fact, take away a three-frame nucleus.

Have your new queen on the centre comb of a three-frame nucleus and put the nucleus into the hive in place of the one removed.

In this way the new queen starts her new life surrounded by her own progeny and does not come into immediate contact with strange bees ; she just carries on as though nothing had happened.

Note that this is done when the bees are flying, so that most of the bees in the brood chamber and in the nucleus are young bees, and such bees can be united without any fuss as they seldom fight.

Alternatively, the new nucleus can be united by the newspaper method.

If we have vicious lots to re-queen they are sometimes difficult ; often they are strong and queens are dark and hard to find, so that removing them may be both troublesome and painful and some of these old tigers of bees just seem to hate the idea of a queen of a different strain.

I generally move such a colony some distance away and let the flying bees enter an adjoining colony, or else just change places with a weaker but docile colony. After a few hours all the tough bees will have gone to their new homes, and we can easily find the queen and remove her, after which the young bees left in the brood chamber will readily accept a new queen.

Chapter XV

CONCLUSION

I HAVE not attempted in this little book to deal with all the many and varied ways of breeding queens, for we may each adopt any method which happens to suit our way of keeping bees. I have, however, tried to set out all the important principles which must be borne in mind if we wish to produce good queens, so that my readers may have a clear picture of what is required, without being confused with methods which are only necessary for the larger breeder.

Queen breeding is not difficult, and I feel sure that if my readers will study the points I have referred to, they will be able to breed excellent queens, and probably better queens than can be bought in the ordinary way. As we produce queens from our own selected strain we can help our neighbour by passing on some of our queens to him, even though they may be old ones, and this may help us too, by reducing the number of stray drones in the area where we hope to get pure matings.

There are many snags and disappointments in queen rearing, as there are in all phases of bee-keeping, but it really is great fun, and can give us many new thrills. I have no doubt that there are many things I have not said for, alas, there are so many I do not know about this interesting hobby, but if you have read my little book and understand it, then you are equipped to start happily as a amateur and make a really useful contribution to the improvement of our bees.

When you have bred queens for a few seasons, you will have an added pleasure as you potter around your hives and see how well your queens are doing. You may, indeed, say with some sense of achievement, " these are *my bees.*"

CHART TO SHEW DATES ON WHICH ATTENTION MAY BE REQUIRED UNDER VARIOUS METHODS

DAY OF ROTATION	CELL STARTING — Queenless bees in colony of breeder queen	CELL STARTING — Queenless bees in other colony	CELL STARTING — Queenless bees in swarm box	NUCLEI — For queen mating	DEMAREE — Demaree for cell building or for cell starting if required	DEMAREE — Demaree of breeder colony for both starting and building
Fill in your own date						
1st		Remove queen from starting colony Insert starter in breeder	Insert starter in breeder colony		Demaree Insert starter in breeder if required	
3rd	Feed ¼ pint daily	Feed ¼ pint daily			Feed ¼ pint daily	Feed ¼ pint daily
6th	Remove queen	Cut out *all* cells				Demaree
7th		Insert larvæ in prepared comb	Prepare box in morning, insert larvæ after six hours		Cut out cells and insert larvæ or	Insert screen
8th	Cells may be transferred to a building colony if desired		Transfer to cell-building colony		Cut out cells and transfer cells from starting colony	Remove screen
10th				Nuclei may now be prepared		
13th		Cells should be sealed			Cells should be sealed	Cells should be sealed
14th to 21st		Transfer cells to nuclei		Cut out cells in nuclei or prepare 24 hours before required	Transfer to nuclei or make nuclei from colony. Filter out drones	Make nuclei or transfer cells to nuclei
22nd or 23rd		Danger of queens emerging			Queens may emerge	Queens may emerge
25th to 27th				Queens may fly		
30th to 35th				Mating probable		
42nd				Queens may be ready for removal